Country Birds
~ Day Book ~

© 1998 Rebo International b.v., Lisse
1998 Published by Rebo Productions Ltd., London

Designed and created by Consortium, England
Production co-ordination: Daphne Wannee, Rebo International b.v., Lisse
Text compiled and written by Cheryl Owen
Ilustrations by Maurice J. Pleger and Dick Twinney (pages 3,11,25,43,65,75,83,101,111,
and 112), reproduced by kind courtsey by Bernard Thornton Artists
Printed and bound in Slovenija

D0257UK

ISBN 1 84053 073 1

Country Birds

~ Day Book ~

REBO
PRODUCTIONS

January

Although common in gardens, the tiny wren is often hard to spot because it scurries with short, darting flights keeping close to dense vegetation. At only 9.5 cm (3 /4 in) long, it has a loud and shrill warbling song that belies its size.

The male wren builds several domed nests of grasses, leaves and mosses. The female partner then makes an inspection, chooses one and lines it with soft feathers. If food is plentiful, the male may be able to persuade other females to live in his rejected nests. Wrens suffer in severe weather and many will huddle together for warmth.

Left, wrens in their domed, mossy nest.

January

~ 1 ~

WOODLAND-LOVER
The green woodpecker is found in all types of woodland but prefers broad-leafed trees in parks and very large gardens, where it feasts upon wood ants and other insects by scooping them up on its sticky tongue. It makes a nest of wood chippings in holes it has bored in trees.

~ 2 ~

~ 3 ~

~ 4 ~

DEAD-TREE RHYTHM
The resonate drum-beating sound that its strong bill makes on a dead tree is very characteristic of the great-spotted woodpecker. It eats beetles, wasps and moths but rarely takes food from the ground, although it will feed from bird tables. Great-spotted woodpeckers do not find favour with bee-keepers since they will raid the hives searching for grubs.

~ 5 ~

~ 6 ~

~ 7 ~

A green woodpecker (top) and a great-spotted woodpecker (below).

M J PLEDGER. 1977.

~ 8 ~

~ 9 ~

~ 10 ~

FEATHER CARE
Birds take great care of their feathers. They are not only necessary for flight but keep the creatures warm too. Feathers are made from a protein called keratin. The birds preen themselves by nibbling and rubbing the feathers to remove dirt and parasites, then comb the feathers with their beaks. They oil their feathers with preen oil from a gland under the tail, to aid flexibility.

~ 11 ~

PEST CONTROL
Green woodpeckers, jays and some other species have a novel method of ridding themselves of feather lice. The birds pound their feet on ant nests whilst quivering their wings. This entices the ants to bite the birds, then produce formic acid which they squirt into the bite. The formic acid kills the lice. This extraordinary behaviour is known as anting.

~ 12 ~

~ 13 ~

~ 14 ~

~ 15 ~

~ 16 ~

~ 17 ~

~ 18 ~

~ 19 ~

~ 20 ~

~ 21 ~

ANNUAL EVENTS
The main episodes in a bird's year are breeding, the moult and, for many birds, migration. They pair up in the spring after elaborate courting and territorial rituals have been performed. Nests are built and eggs are laid and hatched when each species' food is at its most abundant.

The moult follows the nesting period – the birds sing less and loose their feathers which are replaced by new ones. New feathers and plenty of food are needed to prepare them for arduous migration flights or hard winters. Some birds moult twice a year.

January

~ 22 ~

~ 23 ~

CREATURE COMFORT
Unlike their relatives, the great tit and blue tit, long-tailed tits rarely visit surburban gardens but prefer woodland settings where they will roost together at night in family groups.

The long-tailed tit constructs elaborate domed nests from mosses, lichens, animal hair and wool, creating the structure from the inside. The completed nest is bound with cobwebs. Both the male and female work hard in the early spring to build the nests high above the ground in trees and bushes and finish them in time for egg-laying, when the female lays 8-12 eggs. The nestlings are often fed by other long-tailed tits that have failed to build nests.

~ 24 ~

~ 25 ~

~ 26 ~

~ 27 ~

~ 28 ~

~ 29 ~

~ 30 ~

~ 31 ~

The long-tailed tit prefers wooded habitats to gardens.

M.J.PLEDGER

February

Wigeon are social ducks – hundreds of them will gather together to rest on estuaries and mud-flats during the day. They rise rapidly from the water if disturbed and will fly away quickly in tight formation.

The male wigeon has a tuneful 'whee-oo' call which the female will answer with a low purring noise. In courtship, the pairs raise their wing tips and cross them in an almost upright position over their backs. The duck makes a nest amongst bracken or heather, and the drake will stand guard while she incubates the 7 or 8 creamy-coloured eggs. Other pairs of wigeon will often nest close by.

Left, the gregarious male wigeon.

February

BOLD THIEF

Although shy in the countryside, magpies are bold town birds, usually found alone or in pairs. Magpies are generally unpopular birds because they steal the eggs and nestlings of other birds in the spring, although other birds do this too.

~ 1 ~

~ 2 ~

~ 3 ~

~ 4 ~

~ 5 ~

~ 6 ~

~ 7 ~

MAGPIE SYMBOLISM

In Europe, a single magpie is believed to be a bad omen which can be counteracted by greeting the bird. There are various superstitions regarding the number of magpies seen together. Magpies symbolise good luck and happiness in the Far East, where its loud chattering heralds visitors or good news. Native American Indians revere the magpie for its durability.

The graphically patterned magpie features in folklore throughout the world.

~ 8 ~

VIBRANT SONGBIRD
Gaily coloured yellow
wagtails can be found in
both marshland and dry
heaths, moors and
agricultural land, where
they grab at insects
stirred up by the hooves
of horses and cattle. The
male is a particularly
vibrant bird, with a
sharp, warbling song that
he often sings on the
wing. The yellow wagtail
winters in the warm
climes of West Africa. Any
that are thought to be
seen in colder regions in
the winter months are
almost definitely grey
wagtails, which have
yellow underparts.

~ 9 ~

~ 10 ~

~ 11 ~

~ 12 ~

HEAD-WAGGING
Birds that walk rather than
hop, such as wagtails, nod
their heads to and fro
whilst walking. This keeps
their eyes steady as they
walk so they can pinpoint
any food or would-be
predators.

~ 13 ~

~ 14 ~

*A male yellow wagtail in the
foreground with a female behind.*

M.J.PLEDGER

~ 15 ~

~ 16 ~

FEARSOME DEFENDER

The name of the capercaillie is Gaelic in origin and means 'old man of the woods'. With the disappearance of many natural pine forests, the capercaillie became extinct in the British Isles in the 18th century but was reintroduced to Perthshire in Scotland in the late 1830s from Sweden. This hefty bird will defend its territories fiercely, attacking sheep, dogs and people. The cock capercaillie performs an elaborate courtship ceremony in the spring – the males enact mock battles, fan their tails and leap into the air. The male has a strange song that has been likened to a bottle cork popping followed by a grinding knife.

~ 17 ~

~ 18 ~

~ 19 ~

~ 20 ~

~ 21 ~

The glorious capercaillie has a wingspan of over 120 cm (4 ft).

M.J.PLEDGER.

February

~ 22 ~

~ 23 ~

BIG RUNNERS
Bustards are large, well-built birds. They live in open country and, despite their size, are often hard to spot because they crouch low with their heads down if alarmed. Like most birds of the open countryside, bustards have long legs and are good runners. They have a strong flight with slow wing-beats.

~ 24 ~

~ 25 ~

~ 26 ~

DRY-CLEANING
The bustard's natural terrain is quite dry, so it bathes in dust rather than water. The dust is abrasive and absorbent and will scour dirt from the bird's plumage as it ruffles its feathers in the dust. Dustbathing is followed by a preening session.

~ 27 ~

~ 28/29 ~

A female bustard nestles in the undergrowth.

March

Whereas the red colouring of other birds is associated with aggression, this does not seem to be the case with the redstart. These rosy-hued birds are attracted to red objects. The birds live on the outskirts of woods and make their nests in natural holes or hollows and sometimes nestboxes. The female collects grasses and feathers shed by other birds to build the nest, which she then lines with animal hair.

Redstarts make hovering sallies to catch insects in the same way as a flycatcher. They flit amongst the trees and will drop to the ground from low branches to pick up their prey of worms and spiders.

Left, redstarts are active birds that constantly flutter from branch to branch.

March

~ 1 ~

~ 2 ~

~ 3 ~

BIRD OF MIGHT
The golden eagle is a
majestic creature with a
2-m (7-ft) wingspan. It
soars through the sky
above mountainous
regions scanning the
ground for prey, then
dives towards its quarry
of hares, birds or
occasionally young
lambs, reaching speeds
of 155 kph (96 mph).
When courting, the
golden eagle spirals
through the air above its
territory and plummets
towards the ground with
its wings half closed.
Golden eagles pair for
life and make large,
untidy nests of sticks,
bracken and heather
lined with dried rushes
usually on rock ledges,
but they sometimes nest
in trees. They repair the
nests each year before
the breeding season.

~ 4 ~

~ 5 ~

~ 6 ~

~ 7 ~

The golden eagle surveys a mountainous kingdom.

~ 8 ~

~ 9 ~

PRIME PERCHERS
Most birds have thin legs
because the muscles are
at the top of the legs
close to the body. Birds
that perch have three
forward-facing toes and
one long toe that faces
backwards. The weight
of the bird as it lands on
a perch causes its leg
tendons to tighten and
clamp the toes securely
around the perch. This
means they can sleep on
the perch and not fall off.
To take off, the perching
bird contracts the toe
muscles, springing the
foot open.

~ 10 ~

~ 11 ~

~ 12 ~

~ 13 ~

~ 14 ~

~ 15 ~

~ 16 ~

~ 17 ~

SUN BIRDS

It is not fully understood why birds sunbathe. It may be to stimulate the production of vitamin D. Sunbathing birds often look to be in a trance-like state. Some birds appear to simply enjoy basking in the warmth of the sun with their wings splayed open, but since they often pant at the same time with their bills open, it would seem that they are hot enough already. Birds that soar for long periods are prone to bent flight feathers – the bent feathers straighten faster in the sun than in the shade.

~ 18 ~

~ 19 ~

~ 20 ~

~ 21 ~

~ 22 ~

~ 23 ~

~ 24 ~

CHICK TYPES
Generally, newly hatched chicks fall into two categories, nidicolous or nidifugous birds. Nidicolous chicks are nest-dwelling, they depend entirely upon their parents and are usually naked and blind when they hatch.

~ 25 ~

Nidifugous chicks are hatched with downy feathers and their eyes open. They are able to explore their surroundings at a day old when they usually leave the nest, never to return. Although their parents usually watch over them,

~ 26 ~

they feed themselves. Mallard chicks are nidifugous. Mallards often nest far from water, probably because they cannot find a suitable safe spot any closer. It means that the ducklings have a long and hazardous trek to water.

~ 27 ~

~ 28 ~

March

~ 29 ~

~ 30 ~

~ 31 ~

A mallard duckling is quite independent soon after hatching.

April

The elusive quail has a loud call that travels far but it is difficult to pinpoint the calling bird's position. The birds can be found in fields on farmland where they eat grass seeds and weeds.

In courtship, the male circles the female, puffing out and stretching his neck and dragging his wings along the ground. The hen makes a scrape in the ground hidden amongst crops or undergrowth, lines it with leaves or grasses and lays 7-12 creamy, mottled eggs. She tends the chicks alone and they leave after only a few hours. They will fly after about 11 days.

Left, quails watch over a clutch of eggs.

April

~ 1 ~

~ 2 ~

FARMER'S FRIEND
Lapwings are welcomed
by farmers because they
eat harmful insects. They
are thought to anticipate
changes in the weather
and will alter their
journeys accordingly.
Lapwings are highly social
creatures and often flock
together with golden
plovers and other waders
in the winter.

~ 3 ~

~ 4 ~

LAPPING WINGS
The lapwing derived its
name from the
extraordinary aerial
display it performs in the
spring when it climbs
steadily into the air with
its wings making a
lapping sound. It then
tumbles back to the
ground, rolling and
twisting. The lapwing is
also known as a peewit
because that is the
sound of its call.

~ 5 ~

~ 6 ~

~ 7 ~

The lapwing is also known as the green plover or peewit.

April

FOSTERED BIRD

The repetitive call of the male cuckoo says that summer is on its way. The female has a bubbling song, and lays her eggs in the nests of other birds. The host's eggs are disposed of so that the cuckoo nestling has the undivided attention of its foster parents. It soon outgrows its hosts and after a month or two is able to navigate its way alone from Europe to Africa.

The nestlings share their foster parent's diet, but as adults they eat insects and earthworms and certain hairy caterpillars that most other birds dislike.

~ 8 ~

~ 9 ~

~ 10 ~

~ 11 ~

~ 12 ~

~ 13 ~

~ 14 ~

The cuckoo's call anticipates the start of summer.

~ 15 ~

ORIGINAL DUCK
Most domestic ducks are descended from the mallard. They are a common sight on ponds and lakes in towns and cities, and will visit rural gardens if there is a pond there or water nearby. The legs of ducks are positioned towards the back of their bodies, making them awkward walkers, atlhough their legs are very strong for swimming. Flights of mallard can often be seen at dusk when they fly to farmland to feed on cereals and weeds.

~ 16 ~

~ 17 ~

~ 18 ~

~ 19 ~

~ 20 ~

THRILL OF THE CHASE
Mallards have an extrovert courting ritual in the autumn, when several drakes chase a duck through the air, then swim around her with their necks outstretched horizontally over the surface of the water.

~ 21 ~

A handsome male mallard.

~ 22 ~

~ 23 ~

MASTER FISHER
The kingfisher dives for its prey from a low perch or a hovering stance. It beats its catch against a branch, then swallows it head first so that the scales and fins lay against the fish's sides and go down smoothly.

~ 24 ~

COLOUR CODE
The kingfisher is unmistakable with its jewel-like colours as it flits through the air to snatch its prey from the water. The magnificent colours warn would-be predators that the bird tastes awful. It lives on the river bank, lakes and ponds where it catches minnows, sticklebacks, gudgeon and some insects. During particularly hard weather, the kingfisher will search for food along the seashore.

~ 25 ~

~ 26 ~

~ 27 ~

~ 28 ~

April

~ 29 ~

~ 30 ~

The brilliantly coloured kingfisher.

May

Blue tits and great tits are frequent visitors to the suburban garden. They are intelligent, agile birds that are very entertaining to watch. They feed from bird tables and will indulge in skilled acrobatics to get at nuts hanging in bags. The tits nest readily in nestboxes, making their homes of moss and hair. Originally woodland dwellers, blue tits return to the woods in the colder months where they flock together with other tits to collect insects. The great tit's huge appetite for moths and caterpillars makes them popular with gardeners, although they can be a nuisance and are adept at stealing milk by breaking the foil tops on bottles.

Left, blue tits (left) and great tits (right).

~ 1 ~

HIGH FLYERS

Kites are powerful flyers
and will circle effortlessly
for hours above the
wooded valleys where
they live. The pastime of
kite-flying is named after
the tireless style of the
bird. The long bent
wings and characteristic
forked tail of these rare
raptors make them easy
to recognise in flight.
The call of the red kite is
similar to that of the
buzzard.

~ 2 ~

~ 3 ~

~ 4 ~

TREE-HOUSES

Red kites like to nest in
the gnarled sessile oak
trees of valley hillsides.
They construct hefty nests
from sticks, bound with
mud and lined with moss
and animal hair, and
sometimes take over the
abandoned nests of crows.

~ 5 ~

~ 6 ~

~ 7 ~

Although still rare, red kite numbers are increasing.

DICK TWINNEY
© OCT 95

~ 8 ~

~ 9 ~

NEST-INFILTRATOR
The egg-laying habits of the cuckoo, known as brood parasitism, are well known. The female produces more offspring than she can feed, so she hunts out prospective foster parents whilst they are nest-building. Meadow pipits, dunnocks and reed warblers are the main victims.

~ 10 ~

After the host mothers have laid their eggs and flown away, the cuckoo will steal one of the eggs and lay one of her own in its place. She drops or eats the stolen egg. The female cuckoo will lay about 12 eggs in this way in different nests at 48-hour intervals.

~ 11 ~

~ 12 ~

~ 13 ~

~ 14 ~

~ 15 ~

MATCHING EGGS
Cuckoos usually choose to lay their eggs in the nests of birds that have similar eggs. The foster parents may throw the cuckoo's egg out of the nest if they see it as different from their own. The eggs of some cuckoos have evolved to resemble those of the foster parents.

~ 16 ~

~ 17 ~

~ 18 ~

DOMINATING NESTLING
The cuckoo egg will hatch at the same time or sooner than the other eggs in the nest. It will then manoeuvre the other eggs or nestlings into a hollow in its back and throw them out of the nest. The foster parents will feed the assertive young cuckoo, often instead of its own young if any have survived.

~ 19 ~

~ 20 ~

~ 21 ~

May

~ 22 ~

~ 23 ~

BIRD AID

You are not just feeding birds by putting out food for them, but also conserving their energy which they would otherwise spend searching for a meal. This is especially important in the cold months when food is scarce and when they are feeding their young.

~ 24 ~

~ 25 ~

BIRD FOOD

A bird table in the garden will bring a variety of feathered visitors. Kitchen scraps that are high in fat, such as bacon rind, stale cheese, pastry and suet, will be devoured readily. Only put out rice, meat and bones that have been cooked. Grains and seeds are a rich source of vitamins and minerals; sunflower seeds are particularly nutritious.

~ 26 ~

~ 27 ~

~ 28 ~

~ 29 ~

~ 30 ~

~ 31 ~

A male stonechat is so named for its distinctive voice.

June

Canada geese were introduced from North America to parkland in Britain in the 18th century, but many escaped and there are now lots of large colonies. The males and females are similar in appearance, and are 95 cm (38 in) in length. They live on inland water areas where they crop surrounding grassland close to the ground. They also eat cereals and some insects. Canada geese are gregarious birds. As many as 2,000 can flock together outside the mating season. They have a distinctive 'honking' flight and squadrons of geese make long journeys head to tail in a 'V' formation.

Left, a canada goose with her fluffy goslings.

June

GARDEN FINCH
Intensive farming in rural areas has turned the greenfinch into a town bird, and it is now a regular visitor to suburban gardens where it congregates with other finches at the bird table.

~ 1 ~

~ 2 ~

~ 3 ~

~ 4 ~

FRUIT-GROWER'S FOE
The bullfinch has a huge appetite for fruit-tree buds. This naturally has made it very unpopular with fruit growers. It also eats weeds and berries but its short, curved beak with sharp edges for cutting is ideal for quickly devouring the young buds. Bullfinches are believed to mate for life. The colouring of the male is very attractive and the female partner, who is never far away, has a similar but subdued colouration.

~ 5 ~

~ 6 ~

~ 7 ~

Male greenfinch (top),
male bullfinch (centre) and
female bullfinch (below).

June

WOODLAND OWL

It is the male tawny owl that has the classic 'toowhit' call; the female answers 'toowhoo'. It is a bulky owl and has a 1-m (39-in) wingspan. Like most owls, it hunts at night and roosts during the day, usually detecting its prey from its perch. The tawny owl is a woodland owl and is happy in all kinds of wooded environments.

~ 8 ~

~ 9 ~

~ 10 ~

~ 11 ~

NOISY OWLETS

Tawny owl fledglings have a vociferous and monotonous squeak. When they have left the nest but are still close by, they squeak to tell their parents where they are in the hope of being fed. This infernal noise can continue for 3 months – until they can fend for themselves.

~ 12 ~

~ 13 ~

~ 14 ~

A tawny owl perches on a tree branch.

~ 15 ~

~ 16 ~

TOP FLIGHT
The fast-flying hobby is a falcon but can be mistaken for a swift when flying. It is very agile in flight, and twists and turns easily to catch flying insects and small birds in its claws, often eating the insects on the wing. These magnificent flying skills feature in the courtship rituals of the hobby when the male and female circle in the air together.

~ 17 ~

~ 18 ~

Hobbies take over the abandoned nests of crows or sparrowhawks and occasionally squirrel's dreys. The nestlings hatch at the same time as there is a profusion of swallows – a favourite prey of the hobby.

~ 19 ~

~ 20 ~

~ 21 ~

A hobby rests in a conifer tree.

~ 22 ~

~ 23 ~

CHIEF NUTTER
The nuthatch marks its presence with a variety of loud and cheery calls. A woodland bird but also a regular garden visitor, it is prone to show its dominance amongst tits at the bird table where it feasts on peanuts and seeds. Nuthatches make their nests in holes high up in trees and walls. They plaster the holes with mud to prevent larger birds getting in and will do the same to nestboxes, even if it is unnecessary! The nest is built of bark flakes and leaves.

~ 24 ~

~ 25 ~

~ 26 ~

~ 27 ~

~ 28 ~

~ 29 ~

~ 30 ~

The nuthatch has powerful feet to help it grip trees.

July

The snipe's long, straight bill has a sensitive, flexible tip that it uses to probe the mud for worms. When the closed beak is thrust into the soil, the snipe can bend the tip upwards to feel for deeply embedded creatures. It grabs its quarry and pulls it out of the soil without having to open its beak against the resistance of the ground.

As the male snipe dives through the air, its two outer stiffened tail feathers produce a resonate drumming sound. The feathers swing outwards as the bird plunges and vibrate rapidly against the airstream. Although the male produces this sound all year round, it is a major part of the courtship ritual.

Left, snipes are waders and are members of the sandpiper family.

July

~ 1 ~

~ 2 ~

~ 3 ~

COMMUNAL DIVERS
Tufted ducks are highly
social diving ducks. They
flock to Britain and
Ireland from Northern
Europe and Iceland in
the winter, where they
congregate in large
numbers at inland waters
often amongst coots and
pochards. They build
nests in colonies close to
the water and sometimes
on islands.

~ 4 ~

The drake has a long,
dark crest while the
duck's crest is shorter
and she has a brown
plumage. They dive for
food and collect plants,
insects and small fish
from the water. The
ducklings are able to
swim and dive at only a
few hours old.

~ 5 ~

~ 6 ~

~ 7 ~

A male tufted duck.

July

~ 8 ~

~ 9 ~

MOCKING BIRDS
Small birds such as jays, chaffinches and blackbirds will often flock together to taunt a roosting owl during the daytime. This 'mobbing' action is probably territorial – it means that they are less likely to become its victims. The owl is usually forced to move on to find a quieter roosting site.

~ 10 ~

~ 11 ~

HEARING AID
Surprisingly, the owl's sense of hearing is only a little more sensitive than our own but the facial discs of feathers act like a cupped hand against each ear. The position of the facial discs and the ears are slightly asymmetrical in some species, and there are small flaps of skin in front of each ear opening that the owl can control. Owls with asymmetrical ears can hear different frequencies in each ear. So, to catch their prey in darkness, they turn their heads until they can hear the sound of the prey at the same level in both ears. They are then facing their prey and ready to strike.

~ 12 ~

~ 13 ~

~ 14 ~

~ 15 ~

~ 16 ~

~ 17 ~

FOOTSURE

All owls have powerful feet with razor-sharp curved toes. Their short legs are feathered to protect them from the cold and to silence their approach. The owl swoops onto its prey with its feet thrust out in front and its talons open to the fullest extent. It is rare for a rodent to escape the grasp of an owl.

~ 18 ~

~ 19 ~

~ 20 ~

~ 21 ~

~ 22 ~

~ 23 ~

~ 24 ~

~ 25 ~

~ 26 ~

~ 27 ~

~ 28 ~

ROOSTERS

All birds, except owls and some ducks, roost at night. They choose a sheltered spot. Some birds, such as coal tits, roost alone, while other birds gather together to roost. Communal roosts offer some safety since there will always be at least one bird awake at a time to warn of danger, although most birds open their eyes at intervals when sleeping.

Like humans, birds stretch and yawn after resting. Usually they open one wing after another, fan their tails and extend one leg at a time. This is probably to help the blood circulation. Like us, they probably yawn to draw air into their lungs.

July

FEARLESS FORAGER
The coal tit is less colourful than other tits. It is happy in a coniferous woodland where it uses its long, narrow bill to forage for insects and spiders amongst pine-tree needles. The coal tit also frequents parks and large gardens and, given time, will become quite bold with people and take food from the hand.

~ 29 ~

~ 30 ~

~ 31 ~

The coal tit favours coniferous trees.

M.J.PLEDGER

August

Pheasants originated in Asia and were introduced to Europe by the Romans. The males are richly coloured with a 45-cm (18-in) long tail, and the females are dull by comparison. The female raises her young alone and her brown colouring blends perfectly with the bracken and undergrowth surrounding the nest.

Many pheasants are reared by gamekeepers since they are popular game birds, but wild birds breed successfully on heaths and common ground. They fly reluctantly and take off almost vertically if startled, flapping their wings rapidly. When they have reached a sufficient height, they glide away in a straight line.

Left, a male pheasant (top) and female (below).

August

~ 1 ~

~ 2 ~

BEECH-COMBERS
Once found in
abundance, the number
of chaffinches is
declining because of the
lack of hedgerows in
most areas. They are
common in parks and
gardens with tall trees,
and will flock together
beneath beech trees to
feed upon beech mast.
Chaffinches have a sharp
'pink-pink' call and sing
with regional dialects.

~ 3 ~

~ 4 ~

BIRD WALKING
Birds that live mainly
amongst the tree
tops hop when they
are on the ground.
This is similar to the
way they move
between the trees –
jumping from branch
to branch. Birds that
dwell mostly on the
ground, such as the
chaffinch, walk. The
chaffinch has a
distinctive jerky way
of walking.

~ 5 ~

~ 6 ~

~ 7 ~

Male chaffinches (top and below) and a female (centre).

~ 8 ~

~ 9 ~

DRY-NESTERS
During the breeding
season, teals can be
found in peat bogs
and wet moorlands
and they often make
nests far from open
water. In cold
weather, they gather
together on lakes,
ponds and reservoirs
or in estuaries. The
drake has a very
attractive plumage,
while the duck is
mottled brown.

~ 10 ~

~ 11 ~

FILTER-FEEDERS
Most surface-feeding
ducks, such as the teal
and mallard, have bills
lined with rubbery comb-
like plates called lamellae.
Water is drawn into the
mouth and strained
through the lamellae.
Any food left, such as the
seeds of rushes and
freshwater crustaceans,
are then swallowed.

~ 12 ~

~ 13 ~

~ 14 ~

The handsome male teal has a whistling call.

M.J.PLEDGER.

August

~ 15 ~

~ 16 ~

~ 17 ~

PERCHING PREDATOR
The little owl is the smallest breeding owl and can be spotted in the countryside perched on a branch, telegraph pole or a fence at dawn or dusk, its favoured time of day for hunting. They feed upon large insects and earthworms, and will often catch their prey from the perch.

~ 18 ~

~ 19 ~

~ 20 ~

~ 21 ~

The little owl watches and waits for its quarry.

~ 22 ~

~ 23 ~

RARE FALCON

~ 24 ~

Peregrines became very rare birds in the 1950s. They were shot in the Second World War because they were a threat to carrier pigeons, then almost died out due to pesticide poisoning. The birds were poisoned or their eggs made infertile because their pigeon prey fed upon crops sprayed with pesticides. In recent years, populations in Northern Europe have been increasing.

~ 25 ~

~ 26 ~

~ 27 ~

~ 28 ~

SPEED BIRD

The peregrine is the fastest-flying bird, reaching speeds of 275 kph (170 mph) when diving on its prey. The male is called a tiecel and the female, which is larger, a peregrine falcon.

~ 29 ~

~ 30 ~

~ 31 ~

Peregrines on a rocky outcrop.

September

Nuthatches are named for their skill at wedging beechnuts, hazlenuts and acorns into the bark of a tree and hammering them open with their strong awl-shaped beaks. The tapping sound this produces can be mistaken for a woodpecker.

They often attack nuts from above and are as adept at walking head first down a tree as they are at walking up it. Nuthatches explore crevices for spiders and insects and sometimes store nuts in the crevices, hiding them with bark and shreds of lichen. They visit gardens that have mature trees and are often seen in pairs.

Left, nuthatches like to live and feed in tall, established trees.

September

~ 1 ~

~ 2 ~

MASTER MIMIC
The coat of the starling has a splendid dark, metallic sheen which is boldly speckled with white in the winter. The starling is quite adept at mimicking the songs and calls of other birds and even a human whistle. They have a high-pitched squeal which can be heard above the sound of traffic when they roost in their hundreds in cities.

~ 3 ~

~ 4 ~

~ 5 ~

GORGING HORDES
Starlings live in large flocks for most of the year and the sheer weight of the birds can break branches from trees and damage buildings. They are belligerent birds with huge appetites, but the vast number of harmful insects they eat helps a little with their unpopularity amongst foresters.

~ 6 ~

~ 7 ~

Starlings with their spotted winter plumage.

September

NEST CRAFT

Most nests are roughly built, then the bird sits inside and turns round and round, shaping the nest and 'fine-tuning' all the materials in place. The nest must be able to support the weight of its family and protect them from the elements. Most nests are abandoned after one brood, but some species refurbish their former homes the following year.

Mud is mixed to a paste by some birds to bind the nest components together. The nests of swallows and house martins are made entirely of mud under the eaves of houses. Sticks and twigs form the structure of many nests; the basic shape is reinforced with leaves, grasses and coarse animal hair. Man-made materials such as string, baler twine (found on farms) and paper are also incorporated and old nests are taken apart and recycled.

~ 8 ~

~ 9 ~

~ 10 ~

~ 11 ~

~ 12 ~

~ 13 ~

~ 14 ~

September

~ 15 ~

~ 16 ~

NEST WATCH
Take care to observe any nests in your garden unobtrusively. Do not inspect the nest more than once a day when both parents are away, and avoid disturbing them late in the day. If the parent birds are frightened away, the eggs will chill and nestlings may perish in the cold.

~ 17 ~

~ 18 ~

~ 19 ~

NEST INSULATION
Soft materials are used to insulate the nest. Moss is a good insulator. Sheep's wool and animal hair are collected from barbed wire and fences. Many birds use shed feathers – sparrows even pull feathers from larger birds. Lichen and foliage are used for camouflage.

~ 20 ~

~ 21 ~

September

LOW-FLYER
A merlin can be seen flying swiftly close to the ground as it searches for food over open moorland. It holds its head horizontally as it drops to its quarry – this aids its aim on the target. Merlins eat small birds and some insects, and the male will transfer the catch to its partner during flight in the mating season.

~ 22 ~

~ 23 ~

~ 24 ~

BRAVE HUNTER
The female merlin is 30 cm (12 in) in length and the male slightly smaller. They are confident hunters and will go after prey as big as themselves. Merlins make their home on the ground, sometimes in the abandoned nests of crows. Both parents tend their young until they leave the nest after about 26 days.

~ 25 ~

~ 26 ~

~ 27 ~

~ 28 ~

September

~ 29 ~

~ 30 ~

The agile male merlin.

October

The tuneful warbling song of the robin can be heard throughout the year, except in July when it moults. It sings to mark its territory. Pauses in the song allow other cock robins to be heard and so establish a network of territories. Females also have their own territories.

In Britain, the robin is a tame, mostly peaceful character, and has been adopted as the country's national bird. However, it is very defensive in the breeding season and guards its territory fiercely. The robin found in the rest of Europe is very shy by comparison.

Left, the colourful robin is a popular garden visitor.

October

~ 1 ~

TREE-AGILITY
Like woodpeckers, treecreepers have two forward-facing toes and two that face backwards to enable them to cling to the vertical surface of a tree. They use their stiffened tail feathers to brace themselves against the trunk. Starting at the base of a tree, they hop easily up and down trunks and out along branches searching for food. They eat beetles, spiders, weevils and woodlice.

~ 2 ~

~ 3 ~

~ 4 ~

~ 5 ~

SECRET NESTS
Treecreepers nest in holes and hollows in trees and walls and sometimes in nestboxes. The nests are made from grasses, twigs and moss and are often hidden behind bark or ivy.

~ 6 ~

~ 7 ~

Treecreepers cling effortlessly to the trunk of a tree.

October

~ 8 ~

~ 9 ~

BURIED TREASURE
Jays collect acorns in the autumn and bury them in the ground to eat during the barren winter months. They play an important role in establishing new woodlands, since forgotten acorns grow into oak trees and slowly determine new wooded areas. The jay has a distinctive screech which can be heard throughout the year, except when the bird is nesting in the late spring. Jays gather together in the early spring and can be seen chasing one another. They posture and spread their wings and tail as part of their elaborate courtship ritual.

~ 10 ~

~ 11 ~

~ 12 ~

~ 13 ~

~ 14 ~

Its exotic colouring makes the jay a particularly beautiful bird.

October

~ 15 ~

~ 16 ~

BIRD-EATER

As its name suggests, the sparrow hawk hunts small birds. It will suddenly rise and grab its unsuspecting victim and fly away quickly. If its quarry manages to escape, it will not try to catch the same bird again but will look for a new victim. The male hunts while the female is brooding but both will hunt when the young are born, since the 4-6 nestlings produced can eat up to 3 small birds a day. The female is 38 cm (15 in) in length and the male 10 cm (4 in) smaller. Most female hawks are larger than the males and have a different diet so they do not compete for food.

~ 17 ~

~ 18 ~

~ 19 ~

~ 20 ~

~ 21 ~

Like all raptors, the sparrow hawk has feet with long talons.

October

~ 22 ~

~ 23 ~

CLEVER BEAKS
The beak of the diminutive wren is like a pair of forceps, and it can deftly pick up small insects and spiders. The whitethroat is an insect eater too and has a similar beak. The beaks of all birds have evolved to deal with their particular dietary needs. Finches have short, tough beaks to break open seed cases and birds of prey have hooked beaks to tear off meat that is too large to swallow in one go.

~ 24 ~

BIRDSONG
The dawn chorus of birdsong is triggered by light intensity. The earlier the sun rises and the brighter the previous night's sky, the earlier the chorus begins. The chorus is strongest in the courting season – birds sing to attract a mate, to mark their territory and as a warning to strangers. The song dies off in the middle of the day, returns in the afternoon and there is a second more subdued chorus in the late afternoon. Birds sing less in windy weather.

~ 25 ~

Birds also communicate with various calls. Flocks call to one another to tell of their whereabouts when they are out of sight and as alarm signals.

~ 26 ~

~ 27 ~

~ 28 ~

October

~ 29 ~

~ 30 ~

~ 31 ~

The wren has rounded wings and a short, pert tail.

November

Woodcocks make their nests in scrapes in the ground and line them with dead leaves. The female may 'airlift' the nestlings to safety by clutching them between her strong thighs or holding them within her claws if danger is at hand.

The eyes of a woodcock are set high and towards the back of its head, giving it all-round vision for spotting predators whilst eating. Its long, probing bill is adept at pushing into soft ground to search for insect larvae and worms. They often hunt for worms at night when they come to the surface.

Left, a woodcock with its clutch of eggs.

November

~ 1 ~

~ 2 ~

SONGFUL FORAGERS
Blackbirds are clever
foragers of food. They
noisily rake through
dead leaves looking for
insects and will drag one
foot backwards through
the earth while flicking
the soil with their beaks
as they search for
worms. They catch
tadpoles and small fishes
from ponds, and happily
feast on the various
foods put out on the
bird table.

~ 3 ~

Blackbirds have a
delightful and varied
song. The female will
make a nest anywhere
but prefers hedgerows,
trees and buildings. The
nest is very robust since
it is reinforced with mud.
The male will guard the
eggs if the female is
away feeding.

~ 4 ~

~ 5 ~

~ 6 ~

~ 7 ~

Female blackbird (top) and male blackbird (below).

November

~ 8 ~

~ 9 ~

BIRD WATCH
A pair of binoculars are
essential to the keen
birdwatcher. Choose a
lightweight pair with good
magnification and a wide
field of vision so that you
can observe the bird's
environment too.

~ 10 ~

~ 11 ~

NURTURING NESTING
As suitable nest sites
become scarce,
nestboxes are accepted
happily by many species.
Choose the site and style
of box with care and do
not place it in direct
sunlight or towards the
prevailing wind. Position
the box at least 180 cm
(6 ft) above the ground
before the cold weather
starts. This allows time
for the box to weather.

~ 12 ~

~ 13 ~

~ 14 ~

November

~ 15 ~

~ 16 ~

BIRDS ON FILM
Photography is a wonderful way to capture images of your favourite birds. Many nature reserves have hides that enable you to see the wildlife at close quarters. Always enter a hide quietly and have the camera loaded – avoid noisy camera-bag fastenings and talk in a whisper. Avoid using a hide when it faces into the sun unless you wish to photograph silhouettes.

Dusk is a stunning time of day for photographing birds swimming or skimming the surface of well-lit water. Adjust the camera angle to catch the colours of iridescent plumages at their best, and bear in mind that ducks are not at their most attractive in the summer when they lose their flight feathers.

~ 17 ~

~ 18 ~

~ 19 ~

~ 20 ~

~ 21 ~

November

~ 22 ~

~ 23 ~

~ 24 ~

~ 25 ~

~ 26 ~

~ 27 ~

~ 28 ~

TOWN BIRDS
House sparrows are numerous in urban areas where they make their nests in holes or crevices in the buildings. They will nest in nestboxes, often turfing out tits that are already there. The sparrows continue to use the nest after the young have left – it makes a cosy roost in the cold weather.

COLOUR PREJUDICE
Seeds are the house sparrow's main food, but they also feed on insects and scraps from the bird table. Although they are entertaining visitors to the suburban garden, they are unpopular with gardeners because they have an unexplained habit of tearing up yellow flowers such as primulas and crocuses.

BATHING BIRDS
A garden bird-bath provides birds with a welcome drink. It is especially popular in hot weather, when birds bathe to cool down. They pant rather than sweat to keep cool. The bird-bath should be kept free of ice during cold spells, since other natural drinking sources will be iced over too. Birds bathe regularly all year round to keep their feathers in good condition.

November

~ 29 ~

~ 30 ~

Female house sparrow (left) and male (right and below).

December

As their natural deciduous woodland homes have gradually disappeared over the last few centuries, wood pigeons have adapted to live on farmland, although they are not popular with farmers because they feast on the cereal crops. Wood pigeons are also at home in towns, where many are tame enough to be fed from the hand.

They have a characteristic 'coo-coo' call. The male claps his wings in flight as part of his courtship ritual and woos his partner by bowing and caressing her bill. The female builds a fragile platform of twigs for a nest, usually in a tree. She lays 2 eggs and the young are fed by both parents.

Left, wood pigeons in their natural woodland habitat.

December

~ 1 ~

~ 2 ~

BARN-DWELLERS
Barn owls make their
homes in barns,
abandoned buildings and
sometimes hollow trees.
They probably prefer to
nest in buildings since
their plumage quickly
becomes waterlogged in
the rain. Farmers
welcome barn owls

~ 3 ~

because they feed on
rodents. A small window
called an owl hole was
traditionally placed in a
barn to encourage owls
to enter. Farmers
nowadays put an owl box
or barrel in modern
barns for them.

~ 4 ~

Barn owls hunt in
complete darkness at
night. Their ears are
positioned
asymmetrically on their
heads, which helps them

~ 5 ~

pinpoint the exact
location of their prey.

~ 6 ~

~ 7 ~

A barn owl's approach is muffled by its fringed feathers.

December

~ 8 ~

~ 9 ~

MALE GUARDIAN
The female pintail lines a hollow in the ground with grasses, leaves and down to make a nest. The male guards the nest and will distract would-be predators whilst the 7-9 eggs laid are incubated.

~ 10 ~

~ 11 ~

GRACEFUL DUCKS
Pintails are fine-looking ducks. The male has a long, thin pointed tail and attractive colouring; the female has a shorter tail and her colouring is less distinct. They have a graceful, unduck-like walk and will fly away quickly if in danger. They open and close their pointed wings to twist and turn in flight and so make their escape. Pintails dabble at the surface of the water and eat water plants and insects, worms and grain.

~ 12 ~

~ 13 ~

~ 14 ~

The elegant male pintail.

M.J.PLEDGER. 1981.

December

~ 15 ~

SAFETY IN NUMBERS
Partridges roost together in a group, each facing outwards to watch for danger. Like most game birds, they are not keen flyers but will rise rapidly from the ground when alarmed.

~ 16 ~

PROLIFIC EGG-LAYERS
When courting, pairs of partridges will spring into the air and flamboyantly chase one another. They nest mostly on agricultural land that is protected by hedges, ditches or grassy banks. The hen lines a scrape in the ground with dried grasses and leaves to make the nest, and will lay as many as 18 eggs. Many nestlings do not make it to adulthood in particularly bitter weather.

~ 17 ~

~ 18 ~

~ 19 ~

~ 20 ~

~ 21 ~

Partridges have closely-packed downy feathers to insulate their bodies.

M.J. PLEDGER.

December

~ 22 ~

HOVER BOTHER
Many birds hover for a short time to look for or pick up food, but it is a very strenuous activity. The kestrel has a characteristic hovering flight as it searches for prey – its tail fans out and its wings flap vigorously.

When a bird flies, the wings' flapping action and the air flow over them lifts the bird and propels it forwards. To hover, the bird must flap harder and fan its tail to provide more lift. A gentle headwind will help too.

~ 23 ~

~ 24 ~

~ 25 ~

~ 26 ~

HIGHWAY BIRD
Kestrels are about the same size as pigeons. They are welcomed by farmers because they eat rodents and harmful insects. Kestrels frequent farmland, moors and sea cliffs and can be found in towns, where they visit suburban gardens and help themselves at the bird table. They can often be spotted hunting along motorway verges.

~ 27 ~

~ 28 ~

December

~ 29 ~

~ 30 ~

~ 31 ~

The kestrel is a member of the falcon family.

A watchful peregrine.